Original title:
In the Heart of the Night

Copyright © 2024 Creative Arts Management OÜ
All rights reserved.

Author: Ronan Whitfield
ISBN HARDBACK: 978-9916-90-666-8
ISBN PAPERBACK: 978-9916-90-667-5

Twilight's Embrace and Morning's Grasp

In the hush of twilight's call,
Shadows dance and softly fall.
The sky wraps in hues of gold,
A gentle tale of night is told.

Stars awaken, twinkling bright,
Whispering secrets of the night.
Moonbeams weave through trees so tall,
Nature's lullaby, a soothing thrall.

But morning stirs with a bright sigh,
The sun will rise, painting the sky.
Waking birds with songs so sweet,
Life begins, a brand new beat.

Twilight fades, a soft goodbye,
As dawn emerges, oh so nigh.
Yet in the heart, both moments stay,
Twilight's warmth, and morning's ray.

Echoes of a Celestial Whisper

In twilight's embrace, the shadows play,
Soft breezes carry dreams away.
Stars awaken, a dance above,
Whispers of night pulse with love.

Moonlight spills on silent streams,
Chasing softly forgotten dreams.
Each echo stirs the cosmic sea,
A gentle sigh, just you and me.

Beneath the Gaze of Shimmering Stars

Underneath the velvet sky,
Where wishes float and spirits fly.
The stars above, like diamonds shine,
Guiding hearts to intertwine.

Gentle glimmers fill the night,
Creating tales of pure delight.
Beneath the vast and endless dome,
We find our place, we find our home.

A Tapestry of Night's Emotions

Night drapes a cloak of deep blue hue,
   Stitching memories, old and new.
Emotions woven with threads of light,
   A canvas painted in soft twilight.

Whispers echo in the cool night air,
   Secrets shared, a sacred affair.
Each moment cherished, forever spun,
   A tapestry of hearts, two become one.

The Stillness that Breathes

In the quiet where shadows reside,
Stillness whispers, a gentle guide.
The world slows down, embraces the night,
In this silence, everything feels right.

The stars hold secrets, vast and deep,
Inviting us to pause and keep.
In the breath of stillness, we find our peace,
A moment where chaos finds its release.

Mysteries Brought by Starlight

Whispers of the night unfold,
Secrets draped in silver gold.
Galaxies dance across the sky,
Eternal tales that mystify.

In shadows deep, a truth concealed,
By cosmic winds, our fate revealed.
Each twinkle tells a story grand,
Across the void, through time we stand.

Dreams Drift Along the Dusk

Softly glows the fading light,
As day transforms to tranquil night.
Dreams take flight on whispered sighs,
Painting colors in the skies.

Time suspends in gentle grace,
In twilight's arms, we find our place.
Chasing echoes down the lane,
Where hopes and wishes break the chain.

Beneath the Canopy of Midnight

Stars like lanterns gently sway,
Guiding hearts along the way.
Silence wrapped in velvet shrouds,
Beneath the watch of cloistered clouds.

With hidden paths where shadows play,
Lost in dreams that never fray.
Whispers beckon from the deep,
Inviting us to lose our sleep.

Flickers of Light in the Abyss

In the depths where silence reigns,
Flickers dance, breaking the chains.
A spark ignites the darkest strife,
Filling voids with pulsing life.

Moments captured, shadows gleam,
Fragments of a hidden dream.
In the echoes, we will find,
The flame that lingers, intertwined.

Where Darkness Meets the Light

In the shadows where silence dwells,
Flickers of hope weave their spells.
A soft glow breaks the night,
Guiding souls to find the light.

Stars above begin to gleam,
Whispers of an age-old dream.
Through the night, we softly tread,
Following where the heart is led.

Lanterns of Hope in Dusk's Grasp

Lanterns sway on a gentle breeze,
Casting warmth through swaying trees.
They shine bright as shadows dance,
Inviting all to take a chance.

As twilight wraps the world in blue,
Each light speaks of dreams anew.
Hopes arise like fireflies,
Illuminating darkened skies.

Murmurs of the Nightingale

In gardens where the moonlight falls,
The nightingale softly calls.
Her song flows on the evening air,
A symphony beyond compare.

Each note a tale of love and pain,
Echoing softly with the rain.
In the stillness, her voice takes flight,
A cherished serenade of night.

Crickets' Serenade Under the Stars

Crickets chirp a rhythmic tune,
Underneath the watching moon.
Their song a tapestry of night,
Weaving dreams in silver light.

With every note, the world goes still,
Nature's heart begins to thrill.
In harmony, they play their part,
A serenade to stir the heart.

Lanterns Floating in Quiet Waters

Lanterns glow on the gentle tide,
Casting warmth where secrets hide.
Ripples dance in soft embrace,
Guiding dreams in a tranquil space.

Whispers trail with the evening breeze,
Carrying tales among the trees.
Stars reflect in the still, dark sea,
A symphony of peace, wild and free.

Figures Passed in Veils of Shadow

Figures glide through the moonlit night,
Silhouettes cloaked in silver light.
Mysteries swirl where they roam,
In the darkness, they find home.

Softly treading on silent ground,
Echoes linger without a sound.
Footsteps fading, lost in time,
Leaving behind a haunting rhyme.

Heartbeats Underneath Starry Canopies

Underneath an endless sky,
Heartbeats flutter, a lullaby.
Together we breathe in the cool night air,
Moments woven, memories rare.

Constellations tell tales of old,
In their glow, our dreams unfold.
Sheltered by cosmos, we softly sway,
In the dance of night, we drift away.

The Night's Gentle Soliloquy

The night speaks softly, a tender sigh,
Embracing the world as it waves goodbye.
Stars emerge, one by one,
A canvas painted, dusk begun.

In shadows deep, the whispers weave,
Secrets held for those who believe.
Crickets sing their sweet refrain,
In night's embrace, we feel no pain.

Beneath the Canopy of Stars

Underneath the sky so wide,
A million lights, they softly guide.
Whispers of dreams in the cool night air,
Joys and sorrows, we all will share.

The moon hangs low, a silver charm,
Cradling night with a gentle calm.
Echoes dance in the twilight hue,
Each star a wish, a dream come true,

Beneath the canopy, shadows play,
The world fades slowly, slips away.
In this moment, time stands still,
Heartbeats echo with a tranquil thrill.

The Pulse of Nighttime Whispers

Silence drapes the velvet sky,
Stars like secrets flutter by.
A breeze carries the night's embrace,
In this stillness, we find our place.

Moonbeams weave through ancient trees,
Nature's whispers ride the breeze.
A haunting call, a soft refrain,
The pulse of night, a sweetened pain.

Shadows dance in silver glow,
With every heartbeat, we feel the flow.
In the dark, our spirits soar,
The night unfolds, an endless lore.

Solstice Dreams and Starry Realities

As daylight fades, the dreamers wake,
Magic stirs with each heartbeat's ache.
Solstice whispers on velvet wings,
Nighttime breathes the hope it brings.

Under stars, we weave our dreams,
Bright and bold as moonlit beams.
Reality melts in twilight's hue,
A canvas painted in shades anew.

Footsteps quiet on the path less known,
In the silence, our hearts have grown.
We chase the stars, we find our ways,
In solstice nights, forever stays.

A Sojourn Through the Starry Abyss

In darkness deep, we start our flight,
Through a tapestry of shimmering light.
Galaxies swirl and dance afar,
A sojourn through the cosmic star.

Twinkling tales in every breath,
A journey marked by life and death.
Every heartbeat a story spun,
In this abyss, we become one.

Time unravels, a precious thread,
In whispered dreams, we forge ahead.
Stars will guide us on our way,
Through the night till break of day.

Fragments of Radiance in Darkness

In shadows deep, a glimmer bright,
Whispers call, like stars at night.
Each fragment shines, a story told,
In silent hues of silver and gold.

Echoing dreams that softly fade,
Lighting paths where hopes are laid.
Fleeting moments, they spark and dance,
Creating magic in every glance.

Trails of Light in the Night

Beneath the cloak of velvet skies,
Trails of light begin to rise.
Footsteps glow on winding roads,
Guiding hearts where love explodes.

In the stillness, a gentle sigh,
Stars awaken, twinkling high.
They trace the journey we all share,
Filling shadows with tender care.

Azure Hues of Midnight Echoes

In twilight's grasp, the world turns blue,
Whispers flow like morning dew.
Azure notes, they drift and weave,
And in their rhythm, hearts believe.

With echoes soft, the night replies,
A serenade beneath the skies.
Every heartbeat, a vibrant thread,
Binding dreams within our head.

The Nebula of Secret Thoughts

Amidst the stars where secrets dwell,
A nebula weaves its silent spell.
Thoughts like comets, bright and bold,
Paint the night with tales untold.

In cosmic dance, they swirl and glide,
Embracing mysteries, far and wide.
Spaces between, they drift and sigh,
As whispers of the mind slip by.

Twilight's Breath on Ebon Wings

As daylight fades, shadows grow,
Whispers of dusk begin to flow.
A gentle sigh through branches sway,
Embracing night, we drift away.

Stars awaken, pierce the gloom,
Bathed in silver, nature's bloom.
Each flutter is a soft caress,
In twilight's breath, we find our rest.

The nightingale sings sweet and low,
In the dark, our dreams shall glow.
With every heartbeat, time extends,
On ebon wings, our journey bends.

Embracing Cosmic Stillness

In the void, where silence stirs,
Galaxies dance, an echo blurs.
A cosmic quilt, so vast, so bright,
In stillness found, a sacred light.

Each star a point of ancient flame,
Whispers of worlds, they call my name.
Embracing peace, I lose my fear,
In quiet realms, your voice I hear.

Infinity wrapped in dark embrace,
Vastness calls with a gentle grace.
In cosmic stillness, hearts align,
Eternal love, through space we shine.

Silver Linings Against the Night

In shadows deep, where lost dreams hide,
A hint of light, our hearts confide.
Silver linings grace the dark,
With glimmers bright, they leave their mark.

Softly woven through the grey,
Hope whispers low, it lights the way.
Against the night, we'll take our stand,
Together bound, we'll walk this land.

Each silver thread, a story spun,
Illuminates the paths we run.
In darkness vast, we make our flight,
Trusting always in the light.

The Poetry of the Silent Moon

In the stillness of the night,
Moonlight spills with gentle might.
A silver pen writes tales unseen,
In shadows deep, where dreams have been.

Her silence sings of longing hearts,
Each glow a map of hidden arts.
Whispers weave through the velvet air,
In her embrace, we find our prayer.

The quiet speaks in rhythmic tone,
In lunar gaze, we are not alone.
With every phase, her truth unfolds,
The poetry of the night retolds.

Enigmas Wrapped in Twilight

Shadows dance in cloaks of gray,
Whispers weave through dying day.
Secrets linger, softly spoken,
In twilight's grasp, no heart is broken.

Flickering lights, an unseen guide,
In the stillness, dreams confide.
Mysteries in every sigh,
As day bids softly its goodbye.

Time stands still in the dusk's embrace,
Every moment a hidden trace.
Enigmas swirl like leaves in flight,
Wrapped in the folds of endless night.

Stars Sing in the Darkness

In the quiet, stars align,
Songs of light, a cosmic sign.
Melodies hum through velvet skies,
Awakening wonder, softly wise.

Twinkling notes, a serenade,
Echoing secrets that never fade.
Harmonies drift on moonlit beams,
Woven deeply into our dreams.

Each flicker holds a tale to tell,
Of love and loss, of heaven and hell.
Stars sing softly, timeless art,
Touching the soul and stirring the heart.

The Moon's Gentle Caress

Silver whispers kiss the night,
Bathing all in tranquil light.
The moon, a guardian high above,
Watches over with endless love.

Tides of dreams flow and sway,
Guided softly on their way.
In its glow, fears fade away,
Hope returns at break of day.

Crickets sing their lullabies,
Underneath the vast, pure skies.
The moon wraps all in softest grace,
A gentle balm, a warm embrace.

Nighttime's Heartbeat

The clock ticks slow in quiet night,
Every pulse a soft delight.
Stars align, painting the sky,
As shadows dream and moments fly.

Crickets croon their nightly song,
Breeze whispers where dreams belong.
In the hush, the world slows down,
As nighttime wears her velvet gown.

Each heartbeat echoes through the dark,
In the quiet, we leave our mark.
Nighttime wraps us in its care,
Holding secrets lost in prayer.

Reflections on the Water's Edge

The mirror glimmers in the light,
Soft whispers dance on quiet night.
Ripples draw the moon so near,
Nature's secrets, crystal clear.

Beneath the weeping willow's shade,
Dreams of old in silence fade.
Crickets sing the evening's tune,
While stars awaken, one by one.

Footsteps trace the sandy shore,
Heartbeats echo, wanting more.
In shadows, crabs dart and play,
As the tide takes time away.

Twilight's Secrets Unfurled

The sun dips low, a golden hue,
Painting skies with shades anew.
Whispers linger in the breeze,
As daylight bows with such sweet ease.

Colors blend both soft and bold,
Moments caught in warmth and cold.
Glimmers spark the evening's dance,
A fleeting, playful happenstance.

Hidden paths where dreams reside,
In twilight's glow, our hearts confide.
The horizon's edge a promise made,
While stars emerge, unafraid.

Nightbirds in Melodic Flight

Underneath the velvet sky,
Nightbirds sing as breezes sigh.
Their melodies weave tales untold,
In shadows deep, their songs unfold.

With wings that brush the silver air,
They dance in dreams, both light and rare.
Chasing moons through starry streams,
Awakening the night's soft dreams.

Each note a thread, a woven sound,
In the darkness, beauty found.
A symphony of hearts takes wing,
As nightbirds call, our spirits sing.

Restless Souls Among the Shadows

In corners dark, where silence brews,
Restless souls seek paths to choose.
Haunting whispers softly plead,
Echoes linger, hearts in need.

Flickering lights, a ghostly dance,
Through shadows deep, they twist and prance.
Memories fade like autumn leaves,
In search of peace, each heart believes.

The night holds stories, rich and vast,
Of dreams forgotten, echoes past.
Among the shadows, souls unite,
To find their way back to the light.

Murmurs of a Midnight Breeze

In the hush of the night, whispers sway,
A soft caress as shadows play.
Stars above, like diamonds bright,
Guide me through the velvet night.

Trees dance gently, leaves take flight,
Carrying secrets, lost from sight.
Moonlight kisses the silken grass,
In this moment, stillness will last.

Waves of silence, my heart hears,
Echoes fading, calming fears.
Breath of night, a tender song,
In its embrace, I know I belong.

Dreams take shape beneath the stars,
Lost in wonder, free from bars.
Murmurs wrap me, calm and light,
Cradled safe in the arms of night.

Flickers of Light in Darkness

In the depths where shadows creep,
Flickers of light begin to leap.
Glimmers dance in the blackened air,
Hope shines bright, dispelling despair.

Each tiny spark a tale to tell,
Of distant worlds, of dreams that fell.
In the silence, a truth ignites,
Guiding souls through endless nights.

Whispers echo as flames ignite,
Chasing away the depths of night.
With every glow, a heart grows bold,
Stories of warmth within the cold.

Flickers beckon with endless grace,
Carving paths in this dark space.
Together we stand, spirits entwined,
In the darkness, our hearts aligned.

Quiet Reflections at the Witching Hour

The clock strikes twelve, a gentle pause,
As time unveils its hidden cause.
In the stillness, echoes sway,
Thoughts and dreams drift far away.

Reflections dance upon the glass,
Memories linger, let them pass.
In the quiet, truths emerge,
Whispers of the heart converge.

Shadows stretch and softly blend,
In this hour, old wounds can mend.
Light and dark, a fleeting gaze,
In their balance, a soft embrace.

Moments fleeting, yet so bright,
Guiding souls through endless night.
At the witching hour, we bow,
Finding peace in the here and now.

Silhouettes Against the Night Sky

Figures stand in stark relief,
Echoes of hopes, tales of grief.
Silhouettes against the sky,
Whispers of dreams that still fly high.

Stars above, a cosmic trace,
Illuminating each hidden face.
In the quiet, voices blend,
Songs of futures yet to mend.

Each shadow tells a story deep,
Of heart and soul that dare to leap.
In the night, we find our way,
Through landscapes of shadows that sway.

United in this midnight dance,
We seek the light, we take a chance.
Silhouettes join, hand in hand,
In unity, we make our stand.

Breath of the Silent Hour

In quietude, the shadows blend,
Whispers of time begin to send.
The stars ignite a canvas wide,
As dreams and secrets gently glide.

Beneath the veil of twilight's grace,
Soft echoes linger in this place.
A heartbeat pulses, slow and deep,
Embracing all that night shall keep.

The wind, it carries tales untold,
Of ancient paths and spirits bold.
In silence, wisdom starts to bloom,
In every corner, life finds room.

So linger here, let moments flow,
In the silent hour's tender glow.
For time stands still, as dreams take flight,
In the embrace of softest night.

Moonlit Reveries

Underneath a silver sheen,
The world transforms, a tranquil scene.
Each glimmer dances on the lake,
A silent wish, a gentle wake.

The trees sigh soft with stories shared,
In moonlit dreams, all hearts laid bare.
A lover's sigh, a whispered name,
In shadowed light, we feel the same.

The nightingale begins to sing,
As echoes of the past take wing.
Memories weave through radiant beams,
In every corner, hope redeems.

So let us wander through this night,
As moonlit reveries ignite.
In every glance, a spark survives,
In twilight's arms, our spirit thrives.

A Journey Through Shadowed Realms

In shadows cast by twilight's hand,
We step into a mystic land.
With every breath, the darkness speaks,
Unveiling truths that silence seeks.

Each path we tread, a whispered call,
Where dreams and fears entwined enthrall.
The stars above begin to guide,
As we embrace the dark with pride.

Through hidden realms of ancient lore,
We find the essence of our core.
In shadow's grasp, we learn to see,
The light that lives within the me.

So journey forth and feel the night,
In shadowed realms, we find our light.
For every step we choose to take,
Reveals the truth of what we make.

The Embrace of Night's Cloak

As day concedes to night's embrace,
The stars appear, each finds its place.
In softest whispers, shadows play,
Illuminating dreams that sway.

The world, adorned in deepening blue,
Awaits the tales that night will strew.
With every sigh, the moon draws near,
And beckons souls to venture here.

Wrapped in the cloak of velvet skies,
We close our eyes and breathe the sighs.
In peace, we find a gentle rest,
As night enfolds us, truly blessed.

So let the darkness guide our way,
In night's embrace, we dance and sway.
For in this stillness, we belong,
In the embrace of night, our song.

Wandering Thoughts in Midnight's Realm

In shadows deep, where whispers dwell,
Thoughts drift like clouds, a silent spell.
Stars gaze down with twinkling eyes,
In this calm night, the world defies.

Wanderers roam through dreams untold,
Each moment fleeting, yet still bold.
Hearts beat softly, a rhythmic sway,
Guided by night's gentle ballet.

Lost in reverie, I start to trace,
The maps of time, a fleeting race.
Moonlight bathes the thoughts once shared,
In midnight's realm, the heart laid bare.

Yet as dawn creeps in with haste,
I gather fragments, thoughts misplaced.
Wandering minds, now find their way,
As night gives in to the light of day.

When Silence Speaks of Secrets

When silence drapes the world in peace,
Secrets linger, murmurs cease.
A hidden truth beneath the skin,
In quiet corners, whispers spin.

The air is thick with untold tales,
Where every heartbeat softly pales.
In this stillness, shadows blend,
A silent pact that will not end.

Feel the weight of what's unsaid,
In every glance, a thread weaved.
The heart knows more than words reveal,
In silence, dreams begin to heal.

As night unfolds its velvet shroud,
In quietude, we stand unbowed.
Secrets shared in hushed delight,
When silence speaks, day turns to night.

The Dance of Night's Enchantment

Under the moon's enchanting glow,
Stars twinkle high, putting on a show.
Night's soft music calls the brave,
To lose themselves, their hearts to save.

A gentle breeze begins to sway,
While shadows dance and softly play.
In each twirl, the magic grows,
As nature's song in whispers flows.

In twilight's arms, time stretches thin,
Where dreams begin, let life begin.
The world unfolds, an endless trance,
Awash in night's ethereal dance.

Beneath the stars, all fears dispel,
In night's embrace, we weave our spell.
The dance of night, a sweet serenade,
In every moment, memories made.

Moments Lost in Lunar Glow

Beneath the moon, we stand so still,
Moments lost, yet time can't kill.
In lunar glow, our hearts align,
As memories fade, they intertwine.

Each flicker of light tells a tale,
Of laughter, love, and dreams we hail.
In this soft silver, shadows play,
As night enfolds the end of day.

But fleeting moments swiftly dart,
Like whispers lost, they leave a mark.
A dance of time, both sweet and brief,
Each memory holds its own belief.

So let us cherish, ever so dear,
The moments wrapped in night's veneer.
In lunar glow, we find our peace,
As time stands still, our souls release.

Shadows of Solitude

In the quiet of the night,
Where whispers softly blend,
Shadows dance upon the walls,
In solitude, they tend.

Lonely hearts wander free,
Through halls of silent sighs,
Embracing the mystery,
Where forgotten moments lie.

Beneath a veil of stars,
The echoes start to play,
Each flicker tells a tale,
Of wishes gone astray.

Yet in this calm embrace,
A sense of peace remains,
For in the shadows cast,
Hope ever still sustains.

Ghosts of the Shimmering Night

Under a moonlit sky,
Ghosts of dreams arise,
Whispers carried by the breeze,
In shadows where silence lies.

Silvery glimmers dance lightly,
Among the twilight trees,
Each spirit tells a story,
Riding the midnight seas.

The stars, like watchful eyes,
Glimpse tales of yesteryear,
Hopes and fears intertwining,
In the heart's quiet sphere.

As the night slowly fades,
And dawn begins to glow,
The ghosts of shimmering night,
Leave whispers as they go.

A Canvas of Dreams at Dusk

At dusk, the sky unwinds,
A canvas painted soft,
Colors swirl and blend,
As day takes its trot.

Whispers of the evening,
Sing through the gentle air,
Each hue tells a story,
Of moments we still share.

The stars prepare their stage,
With light and dreams combined,
A tapestry of wishes,
For wanderers to find.

In this magic twilight,
All hearts begin to soar,
A canvas of pure wonder,
Forever we adore.

Soft Footfalls on Starlit Streets

Soft footfalls in the night,
Echoing down the lane,
Beneath the starry blanket,
Where dreams and shadows reign.

The whispers of the city,
Flow like a gentle stream,
Each step is filled with stories,
Like pages from a dream.

Lamps glow like silent sentries,
Guarding secrets untold,
In the depth of quiet moments,
New adventures unfold.

As soft footfalls guide us,
Through alleys draped in light,
We wander hand in hand,
Beneath the velvet night.

The Midnight Tapestry Unfolds

Stars twinkle softly in the night,
Threads of silver, weaving light.
Moonlight dances on the sea,
Whispers of dreams, wild and free.

Shadows cradle secrets tight,
Breathing life into the night.
Canvas dark, yet full of grace,
A hidden world, a sacred space.

Waves of silence softly roll,
Nature's heartbeat, soothing soul.
Each breath taken, gently flows,
In this realm where magic grows.

The night unfolds its cloak so wide,
In darkness, beauty does abide.
With every pulse, new stories bloom,
Tapestries woven in the gloom.

Lullabies of the Darkened Sky

Crickets sing their twilight song,
A melody both sweet and strong.
Stars above in hush array,
Guide the weary on their way.

Clouds drift by like dreams in flight,
Carrying whispers of the night.
Gentle murmurs wrap the land,
Lullabies from nature's hand.

Each breeze carries soft embrace,
Time slows down in this calm space.
Moonbeams cast their tender light,
In shadows, love ignites the night.

Hearts will rest, the world will sigh,
Underneath this vast, dark sky.
Time to dream, to let souls fly,
In lullabies of the darkened sky.

When the World Takes a Breath

Quiet moments, still and deep,
Nature pauses, time will sleep.
Gentle echoes fill the air,
In this hush, we all must share.

Leaves are swaying, softly sway,
In the twilight, end of day.
Every heartbeat, every sound,
Calm descends upon the ground.

Mountains watch with ancient eyes,
Guardians of the starlit skies.
When we listen, peace will rise,
In the stillness, spirit flies.

Moments linger, sweetly blessed,
As the world takes a deep rest.
Close your eyes, let dreams take flight,
In the silence of the night.

Midnight's Embrace

Glistening stars begin to gleam,
Wrapped in night like a soft dream.
Midnight whispers low and sweet,
Promises in shadows meet.

The moon's glow bathes the earth,
A quiet celebration of birth.
Silhouettes dance in calm delight,
Embraced by the arms of night.

This hour holds a special grace,
In darkness, find your sacred place.
Eyes closed tight, let worries cease,
In the tender arms of peace.

Midnight's charm, a soothing balm,
In its presence, hearts are calm.
Let the world drift far away,
In midnight's embrace, we'll stay.

The Mystique of Forgotten Hours

Time whispers softly in the dark,
Lost moments linger like a spark.
Memories dance in shadowed light,
Holding secrets of the night.

Each tick, a heartbeat, felt but faint,
Echoes of dreams, a tranquil taint.
Once cherished hours, now a ghost,
In quiet corners, we long the most.

Fleeting shadows, fluttering leaves,
In the past's embrace, our heart believes.
We trace the paths of days gone by,
Underneath an endless sky.

Yet within the stillness, hope remains,
In silent whispers, joy sustains.
For in forgotten hours, we find,
The essence of a wandering mind.

Eclipsed by the Twilight Melody

As daylight fades, a song unfolds,
The twilight's grip in hues so bold.
A serenade of whispers sweet,
Where dusk and dreams together meet.

The stars emerge, a soft ballet,
Dancing in twilight's gentle sway.
Each note a sigh, a lover's plea,
Carried upon the evening breeze.

With every chord, the night's embrace,
Wraps around us, a warm grace.
Eclipsed by moments, soft and rare,
The twilight melody fills the air.

In harmony, our spirits rise,
Beneath the symphony of skies.
Lost in a world where shadows play,
Eclipsed by night, we find our way.

A Gentle Path through Stardust

Among the stars, a whisper glows,
A path of dreams where magic flows.
Through celestial trails, we wander free,
In stardust realms, where hearts agree.

Each twinkle, a journey yet untold,
Beneath the vastness, our dreams unfold.
A gentle touch of cosmic grace,
Illuminating the universe's face.

With every step, we're drawn to light,
Guided by dreams that dance in the night.
In galactic arms, we twirl and spin,
Finding solace where wonders begin.

The stardust whispers, soft and near,
Echoing tales for those who hear.
A gentle path, a love so bright,
Drawing us close in endless night.

Embracing the Spirit of Night

Night enfolds us in a tender shroud,
As silence gathers within the crowd.
The spirit of night, a soothing balm,
Promises peace, a quiet calm.

Beneath the moon, we find our place,
In shadows deep, a soft embrace.
Dreams weave softly through the air,
Tangled with wishes, light as prayer.

Stars glimmer like a distant thought,
In the tapestry of quiet fraught.
Embracing night, we shed our fears,
In the stillness, we find our tears.

The spirit beckons with open arms,
Its gentle call, a world of charms.
Together we dance in twilight's glow,
Embracing the night, as love will show.

Secrets Woven in Twilight

In the dusk where shadows play,
Whispers linger, soft and gray.
Hearts unlock with gentle sighs,
Beneath the veil of fading skies.

Promises float on a breeze,
Carried far by rustling trees.
Hidden tales in twilight's glow,
Written where no one will know.

Stars awaken, dreams take flight,
Shimmering in the velvet night.
Eyes that meet and then entwine,
In this moment, souls align.

The world retreats, just you and I,
Bathed in secrets, time slips by.
In this hush, let silence speak,
Love's soft language, gentle, meek.

Beneath the Silver Veil

Moonlight drapes the earth in peace,
A soothing balm, a sweet release.
Shadows dance in silvery streams,
We find comfort within our dreams.

Quiet whispers in the night,
Wrap our hearts in soft delight.
Every breath, a sacred vow,
In this moment, here and now.

Stars like diamonds, brightly shine,
In your eyes, a spark divine.
Underneath this silver dome,
In your arms, I find my home.

Time slows down, the world is still,
Wrapped in magic, hearts can fill.
Beneath the silver veil we stand,
Together, always, hand in hand.

Echoes of a Sleepless Sky

In the stillness, thoughts arise,
Drifting softly like the cries.
Lonely echoes fill the air,
Underneath the weight of care.

Night unfolds with endless grace,
Stars remind me of your face.
Every heartbeat, every sigh,
Rings like bells in a sleepless sky.

Whispers gather, secrets shared,
In this darkness, we have dared.
Time stands still, the world's a blur,
And thoughts of you begin to stir.

Memories weave through shadowed light,
Painting dreams in the quiet night.
With you close, I feel alive,
In these echoes, we survive.

The Lost Hours of Solitude

In the silence, time slips by,
A gentle breeze, a soft goodbye.
Moments lost in endless thought,
Lessons learned and battles fought.

Pages turn with whispered grace,
Reflections in a quiet space.
Through the stillness, shadows creep,
In this solitude, secrets keep.

Every tick, a silent friend,
Reminds us that our thoughts transcend.
In the echoes, we reclaim,
The lost hours that spark our flame.

Yet within this tranquil sigh,
A world awakens, vast and high.
In solitude, we find our way,
To brighter dawns and hope's ballet.

Wandering Souls Among the Stars

Beneath the veil of night so deep,
The wandering souls begin to weep.
In the vast expanse, they roam so free,
Searching for a place where they can be.

Galaxies whisper tales untold,
Of dreams and hopes that shine like gold.
With each twinkling light that guides their way,
They dance among the stars in playful sway.

A gentle breeze carries their sighs,
As they weave through the darkened skies.
Connected in ways that hearts can tell,
Together they journey, casting their spell.

Through cosmic trails and shimmering dust,
In the embrace of the night, they trust.
For wandering souls find solace there,
Among the stars, they shed despair.

Dreams Take Flight in Darkened Skies

In the quiet hours when shadows creep,
Dreams unfold from the depths of sleep.
With hearts as wings, they rise anew,
Soaring high where aspirations brew.

Glimmers of hope pierce through the dark,
Each whispered wish ignites a spark.
The stars align in a cosmic dance,
Offering the brave a chance to advance.

Wrapped in visions, we chase the light,
Finding courage to embrace the night.
With every heartbeat echoing bold,
Dreams take flight, an adventure to behold.

Across the heavens, possibilities blend,
In this midnight canvas, our spirits mend.
For in the stillness, we find our voice,
In dreams, we weave, we soar, rejoice.

The Enchantment of Lunar Light

Under the glow of the silver moon,
Whispers enchant like a gentle tune.
Lunar beams drench the world in grace,
Painting shadows with a soft embrace.

In the stillness, magic unfolds,
Stories of lovers and secrets told.
The night blooms bright, a captivating sight,
As hearts awaken in the lunar light

Every ripple in the quiet stream,
Reflects the echoes of a fleeting dream.
The moonlight dances on leaves so green,
Creating a canvas pure and serene.

Beneath its watch, the world stands still,
A moment captured, a heart to fill.
The enchantment breathes, a soulful call,
Under lunar light, we rise and fall.

Murmurs in the Stillness

In the silence, soft murmurs rise,
Whispers of secrets beneath the skies.
The tranquil night holds stories close,
Of love, of loss, in shadows, they dose.

Stars glimmer low, a cosmic hum,
Echoing tales of where we're from.
Every heartbeat blends with the night,
Murmurs of dreams taking flight.

Among the trees, a gentle sigh,
As nature speaks, we listen and try.
In every rustle, in every breeze,
Are murmurs of hope that put hearts at ease.

When dusk drapes its cloak over time,
We find our peace in the quiet rhyme.
Murmurs in stillness, a sacred sound,
In the depth of night, our souls are found.

Restless Hearts Awakened

In the quiet of fading light,
Dreams ignite like stars in flight.
Waves of whispers ride the breeze,
Restless hearts seek their release.

Chasing echoes of the past,
Finding solace in love's cast.
Time, a river flowing free,
Awakens souls to what could be.

The moonlight spills across the ground,
In its glow, new hopes are found.
Paths entwined beneath the skies,
Restless hearts, our spirits rise.

With each breath, our spirits soar,
Yearning for what's held in store.
Together, we will dance and play,
Restless hearts guide our way.

A Midnight Reverie

As shadows blend with dreams untold,
In midnight's arms, the world feels bold.
Whispers linger, soft and clear,
A symphony for those who hear.

Stars cascade like silver rain,
Woven tales that soothe the pain.
Each heartbeat sings a haunting tune,
In reverie beneath the moon.

With every sigh, the night unfolds,
Secrets shared in silver molds.
Visions drift on midnight's breath,
A dance of life that conquers death.

In the stillness, dreams ignite,
A canvas painted in the night.
Lost in wonder, we take flight,
A journey boundless, pure delight.

Whispers Among the Shadows

In twilight's embrace, secrets weave,
Whispers float as night deceives.
Shadows dance with fleeting grace,
Hiding tales in darkened space.

Voices linger, soft and low,
Guiding hearts where few may go.
Beneath the stars' celestial gaze,
Whispers lead through life's maze.

A rustle here, a faint sigh there,
Promises hidden in the air.
In the silence, stories bloom,
As shadows play in nature's room.

Trust the whispers, let them flow,
Reveal the paths we long to know.
In the night, our fears take flight,
Whispers weave our shared delight.

The Stillness that Speaks

Amidst the calm, a voice resounds,
In quietude, true wisdom found.
Each breath a moment, pure and clear,
The stillness holds all we hold dear.

Nature sighs, the world unwinds,
In silence, we connect our minds.
Every pause, a gentle nudge,
In the stillness, we can judge.

Hints of life in every pause,
The heart beats loud for love's cause.
In the hush, we learn to see,
The beauty in simplicity.

So linger here, in quiet grace,
Where time and thought find their place.
In stillness, life begins anew,
A symphony for me and you.

A Symphony of Twilight Whispers

Between the trees, the whispers play,
A gentle breeze at close of day.
Stars blink softly, secrets shared,
In twilight's glow, hearts laid bare.

The moonlight drapes like velvet cloth,
Painting dreams, both kind and froth.
Each shadow dances, spirits light,
In this serenade of night.

Melodies drift on cool night air,
Inviting souls to linger there.
With every note, the world unwinds,
In symphonies of heart and minds.

As dusk descends and day departs,
The whispers bind these tender hearts.
In gentle embrace, the twilight beams,
An endless song of cherished dreams.

Chasing Shadows through the Gloom

In the depths where shadows creep,
Silent watchers secrets keep.
Footsteps echo, lost in time,
Chasing phantoms in their prime.

Moonlit paths where whispers hide,
Glances fleeting, hearts collide.
Hands reach out, but darkness laughs,
In the chase of spectral drafts.

Fog wraps tight, a shroud of night,
Guiding souls without a light.
Every corner, twists and turns,
In the gloom, the spirit yearns.

Yet in this dance of fear and fright,
Flickers spark, a fleeting light.
Chasing shadows, through the haze,
We find ourselves in twilight's gaze.

The Nightingale's Choral Reverie

In the realm where night unveils,
A nightingale sweetly wails.
Her voice, a hymn to endless skies,
Melting hearts with lullabies.

Under stars, her melody flows,
Like a river, soft it goes.
Each note, a glimpse of pure delight,
Echoing through the velvet night.

In shadows deep, her songs reside,
Whispered secrets, time confides.
With every trill, the world anew,
A serenade for the moon's view.

Through the stillness, spirits soar,
To the nightingale's sweet explore.
In her song, the magic swells,
In the echo, wonder dwells.

The Wonders that Hide Beneath Veils

Beneath the surface, tales entwine,
Mysteries lost in sands of time.
Veils of silence hold them tight,
Glimmers hidden from our sight.

Each whisper tells of ages past,
In shadows, shadows, secrets cast.
With gentle touch, we pull away,
The layers dull that mask the day.

Within the depths, the treasures gleam,
Unraveled threads of every dream.
Each story waits for hearts to seek,
In veils they whisper, softly speak.

So dare to lift the hidden light,
And seek the wonders of the night.
For in the depths, the gold does shine,
A tapestry of truth divine.

Whispers Beneath the Moonlight

In the hush of night's embrace,
Whispers float on silver streams.
Stars twinkle with a knowing grace,
Illuminating hidden dreams.

Caressing shadows, soft and bright,
The world reveals its tender truths.
In stillness, hearts entwine with light,
As secrets dance in gentle youths.

Through the trees, a breeze does sigh,
Carrying stories from afar.
Silent echoes in the sky,
Love's promise written in each star.

Beneath the moon's enchanting glow,
Whispers weave a tale divine.
In the quiet, feelings grow,
Bound by fate, your heart in mine.

Shadows Unveil Their Secrets

In twilight's grace, shadows creep,
Covering whispers, dark and deep.
They sway and twist, with stories old,
In moonlit night, their truths unfold.

Each silhouette tells tales untold,
Of lovers lost and dreams of gold.
In silence thick, they gather near,
To share the secrets we hold dear.

A fleeting glance, a hidden sigh,
They cloak the whispers of the sky.
Through veils of night, their dance reveals,
The heart's own path, the soul's ideals.

In shadows' arms, we find our grace,
In whispered tones, we seek our place.
Underneath the starlit skies,
We glimpse the truths in gentle lies.

Velvet Dreams and Starlit Sighs

In velvet dreams where starlight gleams,
We wander through a world of schemes.
With every breath, a wish takes flight,
In harmony with the quiet night.

The moonbeams dance on silver streams,
Igniting hearts with whispered themes.
A tapestry of softest hues,
Where love and magic both ensue.

With every sigh, the darkness fades,
As hope and wonder serenades.
Together we write our endless tale,
On starlit paths where dreams prevail.

In gentle arms, we find our place,
Wrapped in warmth, a soft embrace.
In velvet dreams, forever stay,
In love's sweet glow, we drift away.

A Dance of Echoed Silence

In echoed silence, shadows twirl,
A dance of stillness, dreams unfurl.
The heartbeats whisper, soft and low,
As time suspends, and feelings flow.

Beneath the stars, two souls entwined,
In every glance, a love defined.
With every movement, secrets shared,
In quiet grace, we are laid bare.

The night wraps round like a lover's sigh,
In this stillness, we learn to fly.
Every moment, a treasured grace,
In the space between, we find our place.

As shadows dance in soft embrace,
We lose ourselves in time and space.
In whispered dreams, our hearts align,
In echoed silence, love is thine.

Songs of Solitude and Stars

In the quiet night sky, they gleam,
Whispered dreams on silver beams,
Lonely hearts find solace there,
Beneath the vast, unyielding stare.

Songs of solitude softly play,
Echoes of the end of day,
Each star a tale, a silent guide,
In whispered light, our hopes abide.

The darkness wraps like a gentle hug,
A soothing peace, a tranquil mug,
In isolation, we find our song,
With every pulse, we feel we belong.

So let us sway, in twilight's poor glow,
As stars above, in rows they grow,
In the cocoon of the night's embrace,
We weave our dreams in cosmic space.

A Prelude to the Dawn's Whisper

The shadows creep as night unfolds,
A prelude wrapped in whispers bold,
The horizon quivers with gentle light,
As dreams prepare to take their flight.

Each moment stretches, time stands still,
The hearts await the morning thrill,
Anticipation fills the air,
As night surrenders to the dawn's glare.

In soft hues of pink and gold,
The sun ascends, a story told,
The world awakens, free and bright,
A canvas fresh, our spirits light.

So let us greet this new-born day,
With open arms, we'll find our way,
In every heartbeat, hope ignites,
A prelude sweet, as dawn invites.

Silken Threads of Nighttime

Silken threads weave tales so fine,
In the loom of night, they intertwine,
Stars above with secrets gleam,
With every shimmer, they softly beam.

In the quiet, silence speaks,
Whispers dance through shadowed peaks,
Old forgotten dreams take flight,
Spun from the fabric of the night.

The moon, a cradle for every thought,
A silver lullaby gently sought,
As shadows stretch and silence reigns,
We find our peace amidst the chains.

So let us drift on midnight's seam,
Embraced by stillness, lost in dream,
In the web of night, we find our rest,
Each silken thread a calming nest.

Requiem for the Lost Hours

In twilight's grasp, the hours fade,
A requiem for dreams delayed,
Moments stolen by a thief,
Leaving traces of quiet grief.

Each tick of time, a heartbeat missed,
Wishes whispered in the mist,
We mourn the plans that slipped away,
In the dusk where shadows play.

With candles lit, we raise a glass,
To fleeting times that could not last,
In every pause, a silent prayer,
For lost hours, vanished in despair.

So here we stand, our heads held high,
In memories where echoes lie,
For every hour that we have crossed,
Let not our spirits be forever lost.

Mysteries Cloaked in Night's Embrace

In shadows deep where whispers dwell,
A tapestry of secrets knit so well.
Stars blink down, a silent guide,
Through veils of darkness, dreams reside.

Moonlight spills on silent streets,
Each corner holds a tale that beats.
Footsteps echo, time stands still,
In the quiet, hearts can feel.

Riddles wrapped in velvet night,
Beacons glow with ancient light.
A flickering flame, a gentle sigh,
Mysteries woven, never die.

So linger here, in tranquil hush,
Let the night unfold its lush.
For in the dark, the stories find,
A place of solace, unconfined.

Tales of the Sleeping City

The city sleeps, cloaked in dreams,
Beneath the stars, the silence gleams.
Windows closed, the world concealed,
In slumber's grasp, its truths revealed.

Cobblestones whisper tales of old,
Of lovers lost and fortunes bold.
In every alley, shadows dance,
Awakening hearts with a fleeting glance.

The clock chimes softly, marking time,
In the stillness, a hidden rhyme.
Echoes linger, as hopes take flight,
In the depths of the sleeping night.

As dawn approaches, dreams will sway,
What was hidden will find its way.
The city stirs, but for now it waits,
In peaceful breath, it contemplates.

Echoes of Dreams Unspoken

In the stillness, a promise glows,
Of dreams held close, where whispers flow.
A canvas blank, awaits the stroke,
Of desires deep, yet seldom spoke.

Shattered hopes and vivid schemes,
Dance like shadows in our dreams.
Each heartbeat echoes, tales untold,
In every pulse, a wish unfolds.

Lines of fate twist and bend,
In the silence, paths transcend.
The night becomes a veil so thin,
Revealing worlds, where dreams begin.

So fly with thoughts, let spirits soar,
Beyond the realm of nevermore.
In echoes soft, your heart will find,
The secrets locked, yet intertwined.

The Chorus of Midnight Spirits

As midnight chimes, a chorus sings,
From shadows deep, where magic springs.
Whispers rise like mist in air,
Calling forth the dreams we dare.

Figures glide on silver streams,
Woven tales of moonlit dreams.
In their laughter, joy unfurls,
A symphony that twirls and swirls.

Bathed in night's ethereal glow,
Their presence kindles hearts below.
Each note a story, softly spun,
In harmony, we become one.

So heed the call, join in the dance,
Let the spirits guide your chance.
For in this hour, the veil is thin,
Embrace the night, and let love in.

Ciphers of the Starlit Path

Beneath the stars, whispers unfold,
Secrets of night, ancient and bold.
Footsteps trace the silvery light,
Guiding hearts through the shroud of night.

In the stillness, dreams intertwine,
Echoes of fate in celestial line.
Each flicker tells a story untold,
Ciphers of love in the night sky's fold.

With every blink, galaxies spin,
Mysteries weave where wonders begin.
We walk the path, hand in hand,
In this starlit realm, forever we stand.

The universe hums a song so sweet,
In silence, the stars and souls meet.
Together we dance, beneath endless skies,
Ciphers of the cosmos, where eternity lies.

A Symphony Under Dusky Skies

Crickets chirp in twilight's embrace,
Nature's orchestra finds its place.
Each note a promise, softly played,
In the dusk's glow, dreams never fade.

Wind carries tales of days gone by,
While the stars awaken, twinkling high.
A melody swells, the night takes flight,
Under dusky skies, a symphony bright.

Moonlight dances on the water's edge,
A tune of love, a silent pledge.
Each wave a rhythm, a soothing sigh,
In this serenade, we'll softly lie.

As night unfolds with a gentle grace,
We find our peace in this hallowed space.
Together, lost in music so divine,
A symphony under the stars, forever entwined.

Whispers Beneath the Moon

Gentle beams of moonlight shine,
Softly covering paths divine.
Beneath its gaze, secrets reveal,
Whispers shared, we begin to feel.

Shadows flutter as stories play,
Mysteries hidden in light's ballet.
Each sigh a promise, tender and true,
In moonlit magic, I find you.

Stars conspire with the night's soft breath,
Binding our hearts in sweet bequeath.
With every glance, eternity glows,
Beneath the moon, our love only grows.

Soft night winds carry our dreams high,
Under the moon, forever we'll fly.
In this stillness, let our hearts croon,
Lost in the whispers beneath the moon.

Shadows Dance on Velvet Skies

The dusk descends like a painter's brush,
Colors bleed in a tranquil hush.
Shadows twirl in a graceful spree,
Dancing freely, just you and me.

Stars emerge, timid but bold,
Stories written in glimmering gold.
As we watch, time begins to sway,
Shadows dance, chasing night away.

Every heartbeat, a soft refrain,
Under velvet skies, love's sweet gain.
In the twilight, dreams take their flight,
Carried on whispers of the night.

Together, we weave a tapestry bright,
In this moment, everything feels right.
As shadows dance in cosmic embrace,
We'll find our rhythm in this endless space.

Secrets of the Starry Veil

In whispers soft, the night unfolds,
The secrets that the starry veil holds.
Each twinkle tells of dreams and fears,
Unraveled slowly through the years.

Beneath the moon's gentle, watchful glow,
Where shadows dance and wild winds blow.
A tapestry of cosmic lore,
Invites the hearts of those who explore.

The universe hums a tender tune,
As stardust drifts from silvery moon.
In this vast realm of wonder and grace,
We find our truths in the infinite space.

So, gaze above, let thoughts take flight,
For the stars guard secrets of the night.
With every blink, new stories arise,
Beneath the spell of the endless skies.

Dreamscapes in Dusk's Embrace

When dusk descends with a velvet sigh,
The world transforms beneath the sky.
Shadows stretch and colors blend,
In dreamscapes where the heart can mend.

Soft whispers linger on the breeze,
As daylight fades among the trees.
A tranquil hush blankets the land,
While twilight weaves with a gentle hand.

Here, time pauses, a fleeting kiss,
Each moment a fragment of bliss.
In the twilight's soft, golden grace,
We dance in dreams, finding our place.

So let your spirit soar and glide,
On dusk's embrace, take a wild ride.
In every corner, magic awaits,
In the dreamscapes crafted by fates.

Midnight Serenade for the Forgotten

In the silence of midnight's hold,
Echoes linger, tales untold.
A serenade for souls lost near,
Whispers of love, tinged with fear.

Stars flicker like candles burned low,
Guiding the way for the hearts that flow.
Through the shadows of memories past,
A melody plays, a spell is cast.

With each note, a memory sighs,
Carried on winds under darkened skies.
The forgotten find solace in song,
As night carries notes where they belong.

So listen close as the world drifts away,
To the midnight serenade, let us sway.
Embrace the whispers, and never forget,
The love that lingers in the silhouettes.

The Lullaby of Silent Hours

When the clock strikes the hour of peace,
A lullaby sings as worries cease.
In the silence, the heart beats slow,
Wrapped in dreams, we gently flow.

The world outside fades to a hush,
Where shadows dance in twilight's blush.
Stars peer down through the darkened space,
Cradling us in their soft embrace.

Each note whispers of love and light,
Carrying hopes through the calm of night.
In the stillness, we find our home,
Guided by the lullabies that roam.

So rest your head and close your eyes,
Let the silent hours serenely rise.
In a world where dreams convene,
Embrace the magic of the unseen.

Milton Keynes UK
Ingram Content Group UK Ltd.
UKHW022337011124
450602UK00005B/67